The New Circus

Written by Charles Knutter
Illustrated by Ashley Knutter

DORRANCE
PUBLISHING CO
EST. 1920
PITTSBURGH, PENNSYLVANIA 15238

Dorrance Publishing Co
585 Alpha Drive
Pittsburgh, PA 15238
Visit our website at *www.dorrancebookstore.com*

ISBN: 978-1-6453-0097-7
eISBN: 978-1-6453-0063-2

The New Circus

When our hunter-gatherer ancestors, given the sedentary benefits of innovations in mostly agriculture and domestication but also tempered with the sobering realization of impending death, no longer had to spend every waking moment surviving were inevitably driven to consider their existence. From this sprang myths, religions, ideologies, and a lineage of thinkers from Socrates to Monty Python (in the west) searching for the meaning of life. Along the way was created the Political Spectrum: with Liberals left of center and Conservatives right of center and increasingly extremer versions of each continuing out away from the moderate center.

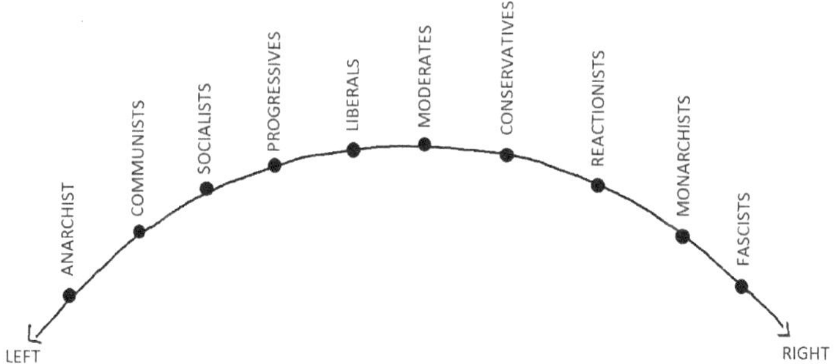

This process had been evolving for thousands of years, but the coupling of ideology with political parties has been a recent development because political parties are a recent development. Although our first political party system would appear at the end of the 1700s, Federalists vs. Anti-Federalists, this was largely a clash between Alexander Hamilton and Thomas Jefferson and how they each envisioned the role of the world's only republic. It was later, in the 1830s, less than 200 years ago, when our second party system, this time Democrats vs. Whigs, would become the world's first truly modern party system; e.g. with conventions, running mates, the popular vote etc. And that was decades before it would appear anywhere else.

Not unlike the hunter-gatherers of the past, freed from their mundane daily chores, thoughtful individuals today, based on personal experiences, observations, and education, decide where they fall on the Political Spectrum. As from the writings of Thomas Hobbes, those on the left tend to distrust human nature and look to a strong central government to ensure the welfare of mankind. Opposed to Hobbes, those on the right follow the laissez faire teachings of Hobbes' fellow Englishman, John Locke, who felt that people were basically good and should have a minimum of governing in their lives.

It is well known that with youth comes the ability to accept change, to adapt, a tool evolved to move humans forward. But, with age comes a stubborn urge to protect and maintain the status quo, a justification for a commitment and investment in a way of life. It was, after all, the older generation of Soviet bloc citizens who most resisted the fall of Communism, fearful of what lay ahead and abhorred to admit that the best years of their lives had been spent under a failed system. And as a result, creating Putin, the international poster child for reactionary politics, a conservative response to the loss of an extreme left-wing regime. (In fact, the great leftist international threat of Communism from the former Soviet Union and today from China has always been dictated by a handful of nationalistic and conservative old men. The only difference being that the Russians were committed to a Marxist economic model while trying to compete with the west, morally and militarily, and went belly up, whereas the Chinese are more than willing to play a dictatorial form of Capitalism, without the bothersome checks and balances and the free press that our founders so wisely installed for us.)

Here today, we find ourselves in a party system in which each party appears wholly entrenched on opposite sides of the political spectrum. Historically, the battle between Liberals and Conservatives had been just as contentious within the Parties as it is now between the Parties. In the election of 1972, President Nixon, a conservative Republican, faced primary challenges from the liberal Congressman, Paul McCloskey. On the Democratic side, you had Liberals like Edmund Muskie and George McGovern on the same ballot with the ultra-Conservative George Wallace. Sensing the on-coming realignment, candidate John Lindsay, the liberal Republican mayor of New York City switched to the Democratic Party prior to the campaign. Today, a liberal Republican or a conservative Democrat is a rare sight.

What must be understood is that through time and each succeeding Party System, the platforms of the Parties change, but the principles of Conservatism and Liberalism have remained constant. For example, it was the Democratic Party of the late 1800s and early 1900s, dominated by southern Conservatives, unable to win hearts and minds through intelligent persuasion, that resorted to voter suppression. This they accomplished with poll taxes, literacy tests, grandfather clauses, and outright intimidation. Today, it's the Republican Party, dominated by Conservatives, who've decided that in order to gain and hold power they too must keep certain people from voting. This they've accomplished by requiring IDs, long voter lines, the war on drugs, revoking registration through an array of undemocratic voter purging schemes, or just skewing the outcome through gerrymandering. The political parties had overtime changed, but the Conservative necessity to disenfranchise voters has not.

It was in the early 1900s that liberal and moderate Republicans, working with Republican President Theodore Roosevelt, pushed through Congress a Progressive agenda: regulating monopolies, railroads, drugs, food, child labor, creating the Forest Service and putting under protection over 275,000 sq. miles of federal lands, including the Grand Canyon, Devil's Tower, Mt. Olympus, and more. Now, Liberals stand in opposition to today's Republican President who has removed protections from national monuments (favoring oil interests over those of Native Americans), taken the U.S. out of the Paris climate deal, scoffs at climate change, promotes the burning of coal, and has gutted the E.P.A. Two Presidents, both Republicans, as different as night and day, one working with Liberals to protect the environment, and the other determined to stop Liberals from protecting the environment.

It might help to understand the Conservative approach to the environment by examining the distinction between materialists and idealists, the two main schools of philosophic thought. Broadly speaking, Conservatism is in step with the idealist belief that all the stuff of life, all matter, is the result of the mind, whereas Liberals lean to the materialistic view that from matter would flow all ideas. To the idealist the universe is a manifestation of the mind and to be regarded as such. Materialists make the effort to move away from revelation and miracles, and instead look to a science-based method, and therefore view nature as precious and irreplaceable and more than just a source of profit.

> "Come, come my conservative friend, wipe the dew
> off your spectacles, and see that the world is moving."
> Elizabeth Cady Stanton.

"Conservative, n. A statesman who is enamored of existing evils, as distinguished from the Liberal, who wishes to replace them with others."

Ambrose Bierce.

"The radical of one century is the conservative of the next."

Mark Twain.

"A love of tradition has never weakened a nation, indeed it has strengthened nations in their hour of peril; but the new view must come, the world must roll forward."

Sir Winston S. Churchill.

"The liberals in the House strongly resemble liberals I have known through the last two decades in the civil rights conflict. When it comes time to show on which side they will be counted, they suddenly excuse themselves."

Shirley Chisholm.

"When a nation's young men are conservative, its funeral bell is already rung."

Henry Ward Beecher.

The New Circus

In the spring of 2017, we Americans saw the retirement of one of the more colorful patches of our cultural quilt when the Ringling Brothers circus, pride of Baraboo and Sarasota, put on its final performance and then pulled up stakes for the last time. Although long treasured for providing a stage for amazing performers while creating a multitude of various employment opportunities, the real beauty and the True Purpose of the circus was its delivering of quality entertainment to all, indiscriminately, at a fair price.

Unlike politics, the wonder and enchantment of the circus was best seen through the eyes of a child, naïve and unwary. However, when such criteria is applied to a Presidential election, "the last best hope of earth" may awaken to find that the greatest threat to that very hope, with his shallow instincts and privileged world view, now resides at 1600 Pennsylvania Avenue.

All of which begs for a little circus story…

Once upon a time, long ago and far away, in an old world, it was the circus animals themselves that managed the show:

There was a well-traveled and innovative circus of the Lions.

And there was a massive and powerful circus of the Bear.

And there was even a circus that was run with the Bulls.

Among others.

With the passing of seasons, these olden day circuses would lose sight of their True Purpose, and increasingly, unable to resolve inward, they projected outward. Without consideration for the needs of their own audience, these circuses turned on their circus neighbors, meddling and/or occupying. As the attention of these circuses turned elsewhere, it caused a detriment of quality entertainment at home until the circus-goers had reached an impasse…

What to do?

Realizing that they had become the captive audience of circuses lacking tolerance and potential, they acted. Now, several of these affected and rejected groups began to cross over to the other side of the big pond to create a new kind of circus; one that would never forget its True Purpose, one that would always remember to mind its own business, and one that would never feature Lions, Bears or Bulls.

Unencumbered by old world restraints, the New Circus took shape, benefiting from the collective efforts of self-motivation.

But with the approaching of opening day, a problem arose: those working alongside the fledgling Donkeys to develop the sunny side of the circus wouldn't rely on self-motivation, insisting that a segment of their labor force needed to be kept in perpetual and forced motivation. Although they felt this was a peculiar violation of what the New Circus stood for, the rest of the circus reluctantly agreed because…The Show Must Go On!

Soon the Donkey performance would emerge as the most popular attraction of the circus, ushering in an era-of-good-circus-feeling. Yet, as one successful season followed the next, the stubborn Donkeys refused to release their subjugated laborers and instead moved to expand their peculiar labor practices into other areas of the circus!

Meanwhile, as the Donkey was pressing his transgression, there was founded in a rippin' area of the New Circuses' Dairyland, a troupe of Elephants, whose performance quickly began to draw large crowds. Now, feeling threatened the Jack-ass Donkey swore he'd split the circus in half and ruin all they had built and achieved.

Having used up all of their compromises, the two camps prepared for Civil War. Initially the Donkey and his troops saw brilliant success, but eventually the Elephant would bring his great weight and superior resources to bear down on the Donkeys, forcing them to surrender and to accept that there would be a grand re-opening of the New Circus based on the rule of freedom and equal opportunity for all; a fulfillment of the original promise!

Embittered by the violence and upheaval wrought by conflict, there were those who sought to vent their anger. Fortunately for all concerned there was one, among a few, who understood the magnitude of what had passed. It was their most "Able" Elephant patriarch who had gained the wisdom to see that only compassion and forgiveness would ever get the New Circus up and morally profitable again.

Just as the roar of the guns drew silent and as the dust settled down on the wrecked circus, a crazed and partisan supporter of the Donkey crept into the Elephant quarters and murdered the beloved leader. At that moment any chance for a smooth and thoughtful reconciliation for the New Circus was lost.

Luckily for the Elephant fan base, the Grand Old Patriarch had two capable sons: one played a Stalwart character, conservative by nature, the other had a more Radical, and then Progressive, role to play. Now, driven by rage, they moved to occupy the Donkey tents as they simultaneously championed the formerly enslaved laborers while fermenting hatred from the Donkeys, stampeding and harassing and endlessly waving their bloody red flags.

This had gone on for just a few short seasons when to everyone's amazement the just recently defeated Donkeys were already attracting the larger crowds and demanding the big top! This was unacceptable to the Elephant brothers, so they offered a solution: If the Donkeys would acknowledge the Elephant as the "main" attraction, for the unforeseen future, they would put away their bloody red flags, pack-up, and let the Donkeys deal with the recently freed workers in a manner of their own choosing. So, the Donkeys, and their new friend, Jim the Crow, headed home to do just that.

Unfettered, the Elephants went about monopolizing circus resources and making war on the neighboring Buffalo to the west, as a means to take their ground, continuing a plot-line and a trail of tears not unlike that performed by an earlier Donkey (the one on your $20 bill). So, the torch had been passed, and soon the Buffalo would be driven near to extinction.

This arrangement continued for several seasons until, lacking any real competition, the two Elephant brothers began to butt heads over the direction of the New Circus. Then, after sitting down to a particularly yellow "journalistic" serving of hay, the brother that had always stood to the right decided that it was time for the New Circus to force its brand of circus management onto some other mismanaged circuses (for their own higher good). For a short time, the New Circus could revel in overseas victories, but in the long run he had accomplished nothing but putting the stain of "imperialistic" hypocrisy on the New Circus and instilling an animosity among some of the world's circus goers that lingers to this day. This Elephant had forgotten. Dismayed and increasingly irrelevant, his Progressive brother would soon be seen walking off into the distance, a faded memory.

And as for the remaining brother? He reacted by isolating himself from the realities of the circus world.

Elephants often display Ostrich envy.

Now, with unbridled enthusiasm, several scattered bands of Donkeys, and their teamsters, began to organize, announcing they had a "new deal" for all the performers, laborers, and circus-goers alike. And later, as these developments threatened to lead to a "great society," it prompted one exceptionally tricky Elephant to come up with a strategy to slip down and explain to the Donkey base that they, and their specific needs, would be much better served under a new and improved Elephant facility, to which they agreed. Soon the original Donkey breed would all but disappear from its homeland, until there was Nunn left.

To the casual circus critic, it would have seemed inevitable that the New Circus would have been in a position of dominance for several seasons to come. With its boundless amenities, reservoir of New Circus converts, and the continual sacrifices of some of its "Greatest" attendees, the New Circus should have been at its pre-eminence, but something had gone wrong.

Having lost its center, the New Citcus began to lose its reputation as a trend setter, and instead fell into debt and disrepair. Something had to change, or the New Circus would go bankrupt. So, representatives of all the various groups of the circus went to see the Donkeys, but the Donkeys had lost their voice, and besides, they could only stir up interest in their performance every fourth season, and that obviously wasn't enough to make an impact at the gate.

So, the representatives of the various groups of the circus trekked all the way to the extreme other end of the circus to see the Elephants. There, they found them with their close ally, the cunning Fox, but the Elephants, although by now they had secured the vast share of the circus, had grown angry and paranoid, and anyway, it had become apparent that the Elephant's performance was really only meant to entertain a select few.

The circus-goers had reached an impasse.

What to do?

Finally, after several minutes of reflection, someone yelled out, "Maybe we should never have put these animals in charge of the circus in the first place!"

Then someone added, "Yeah, we might just as well put a Clown in charge of the circus!"

After quite a while, when the laughter had finally subsided, it became clear that the speaker was serious; in fact, he wasn't alone. And although the majority thought it was insane to put a Clown in charge of the circus, they had underestimated the overwhelming angst of the others, who were willing to take the risk, as if they had been swayed by a rush of misinformation.

So, that's how a Clown was put in charge of the New Circus, and from a Clown, outrageous and manipulative behavior can be expected, because that's his real talent. (With a wink and a nod to those infamous handlers, Goebbels and Roy.)

Throughout its history, several Clowns have aspired to lead the New Circus: anti-immigrant, anti-Catholic, anti-Semitic, Communists, racists, billionaires, and other Know-Nothings, until now, all relegated to the path of the third-party, an effective dead-end. They serve as a valuable gauge, an indicator on the spectrum of our political conscience, as a dire forewarning of the lurking desires of the worse angels of our nature.

Having accomplished its hostile takeover of the Elephant's stage, has the Clown transformed the Elephant, or will the Elephant find the integrity to withstand him? One thing is certain: they've long forgotten the Progressive values of their greatest leaders; that Elephant's grave marker is carved into the side of a mountain in the Black Hills.

In the spring of 2017, America would lose more than just one class act. Damn that 22nd Amendment, anyway.

♪ ♫ ♪ ♫ FOR THE BENEFIT OF
MR. KOCH THERE WILL BE
A SHOW TONITE . . .
WHEN
PEDRO
SHRUGGED

CLIMATE
?
WHAT
CLIMATE

PACK
THE
HOUSE
By Jerry Mander

The End

"To announce that there must be no criticism of the President or that we are to stand by the President, right or wrong, is not only unpatriotic and servile, but is morally treasonable to the American people."

Theodore Roosevelt

"My people are destroyed by the lack of knowledge, because thou hast rejected knowledge I will also reject thee."

Hosea

"Whence shall we expect the approach of danger? Shall some trans-Atlantic giant step the earth and crush us at a blow? Never. All the armies of Europe and Asia could not by force take a drink from the Ohio River or make a track on the Blue Ridge in the trial of a thousand years. If destruction be our lot, we must ourselves, be its author and finisher. As a nation of free men we will live forever or die by suicide."

Abraham Lincoln

"Verily, God is Compassionate and is fond of compassion, and He gives to the compassionate what He does not give to the harsh."

Prophet Muhammad

"Here is your country. Cherish these natural wonders, cherish these natural resources, cherish the history and romance as a sacred heritage, for your children and your children's children. Do not let selfish men or greedy interests skin your country of its beauty, its riches or its romance."

Theodore Roosevelt.

TRUMP
2020